T0396006

A DAY IN THE LIFE OF A
SCIENTIST

THIS EDITION

Produced for DK by WonderLab Group LLC
Jennifer Emmett, Erica Green, Kate Hale, *Founders*

Editor Maya Myers; **Photography Editor** Kelley Miller; **Managing Editor** Rachel Houghton;
Designers Project Design Company; **Researcher** Michelle Harris; **Copy Editor** Lori Merritt;
Indexer Connie Binder; **Proofreader** Susan K. Hom; **Series Reading Specialist** Dr. Jennifer Albro

First American Edition, 2025
Published in the United States by DK Publishing, a division of Penguin Random House LLC
1745 Broadway, 20th Floor, New York, NY 10019

A catalog record for this book is available from the Library of Congress.
HC ISBN: 978-0-5939-6248-0
PB ISBN: 978-0-5939-6247-3

DK books are available at special discounts when purchased in bulk for sales promotions, premiums, fund-raising,
or educational use. For details, contact:
DK Publishing Special Markets, 1745 Broadway, 20th Floor, New York, NY 10019
SpecialSales@dk.com

Printed and bound in China
Super Readers Lexile® levels 310L to 490L
Lexile® is the registered trademark of MetaMetrics, Inc. Copyright © 2024 MetaMetrics, Inc. All rights reserved.

The publisher would like to thank the following for their kind permission to reproduce their images:
a=above; c=center; b=below; l=left; r=right; t=top; b/g=background
Alamy Stock Photo: Associated Press / Michael Macor 17, Mountain Light / Galen Rowell 7t, NatPar Collection 8,
Natural History Collection 10cr, NPS Photo 28, Science History Images 23cra, Anton Sorokin 7cr, 30tl,
SuperStock / RGB Ventures / Jim Reed 18-19t; **Dreamstime.com:** Aaron Amat 24br, 30clb, Yuri Arcurs 3, 9cra,
Rafael Ben Ari 15, Buranatrakul 29tl, Chernetskaya 10tr, Dragoscondrea 29tr, Aleksei Gorodenkov 9tl, 30cl, Moose
Henderson 10c, Roberto Junior 20bl, Michael Klenetsky 12tl, Pressmaster 11, Pablo Hidalgo / Pxhidalgo 23tc, 30bl,
Rawpixelimages 12ca, Yekaixp 22; **Getty Images:** E+ / Fotostorm 6, E+ / Lucentius 26, E+ / Technotr 4-5, Tongpool
Piasupun 16, Wanderluster 20br, Evgeniy Kharitonov 23cla; **NASA:** ESA 27br, JPL-Caltech 27tl; **NPS:** David Tomeo
13; **Science Photo Library:** MSF / Javier Trueba 21, Philippe Psaila 1, Volker Steger 25bl, 25b, 30cla;
Shutterstock.com: BearFotos 24cl; U.S. **Geological Survey:** 14

Cover images: *Front:* **Dreamstime.com:** Visual Generation (Background); **Getty Images / iStock:** E+ / Alvarez;
Back: **Dreamstime.com:** Cat Vec cra/ (clb)

www.dk.com

A DAY IN THE LIFE OF A
SCIENTIST

Ruth A. Musgrave

Contents

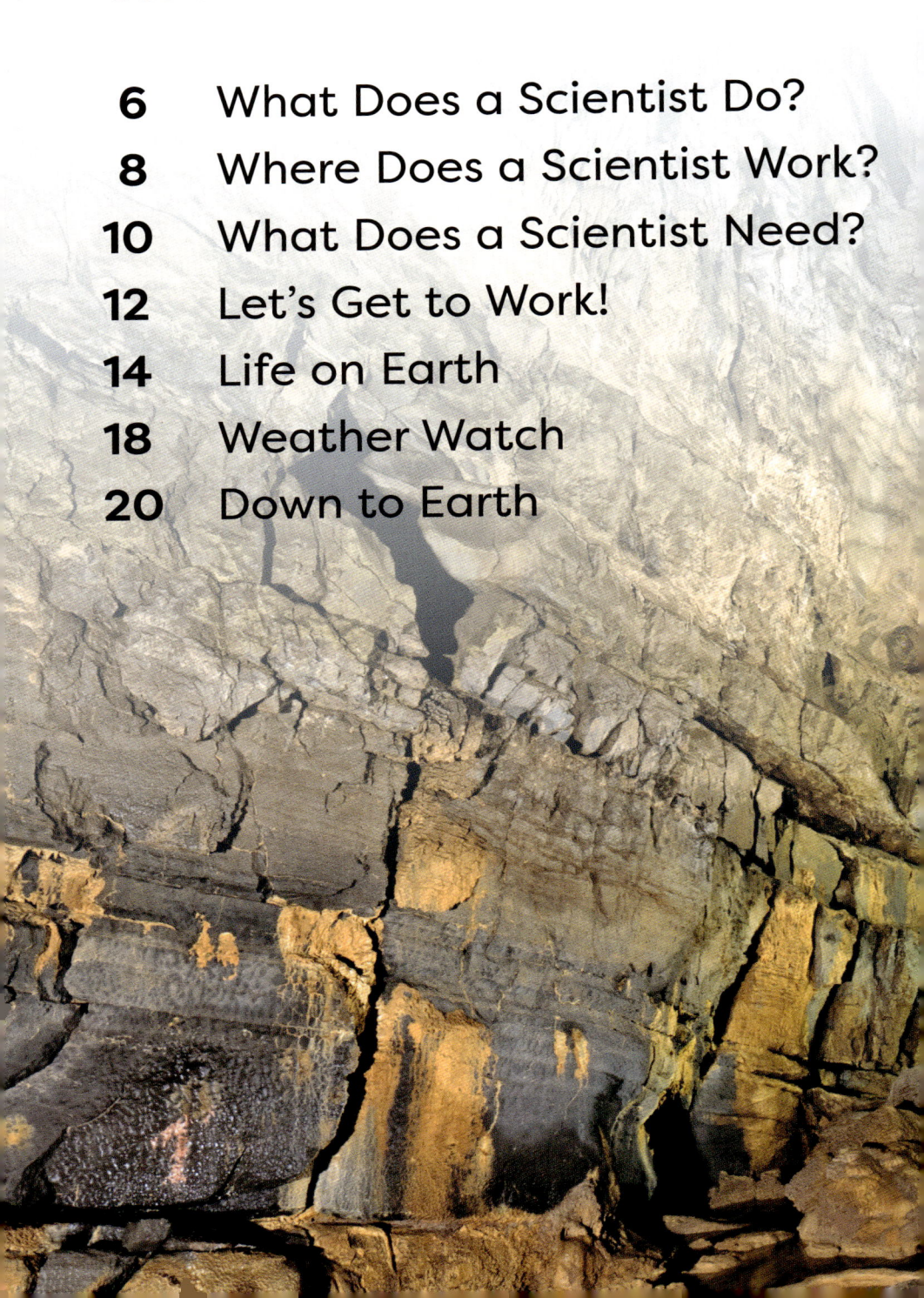

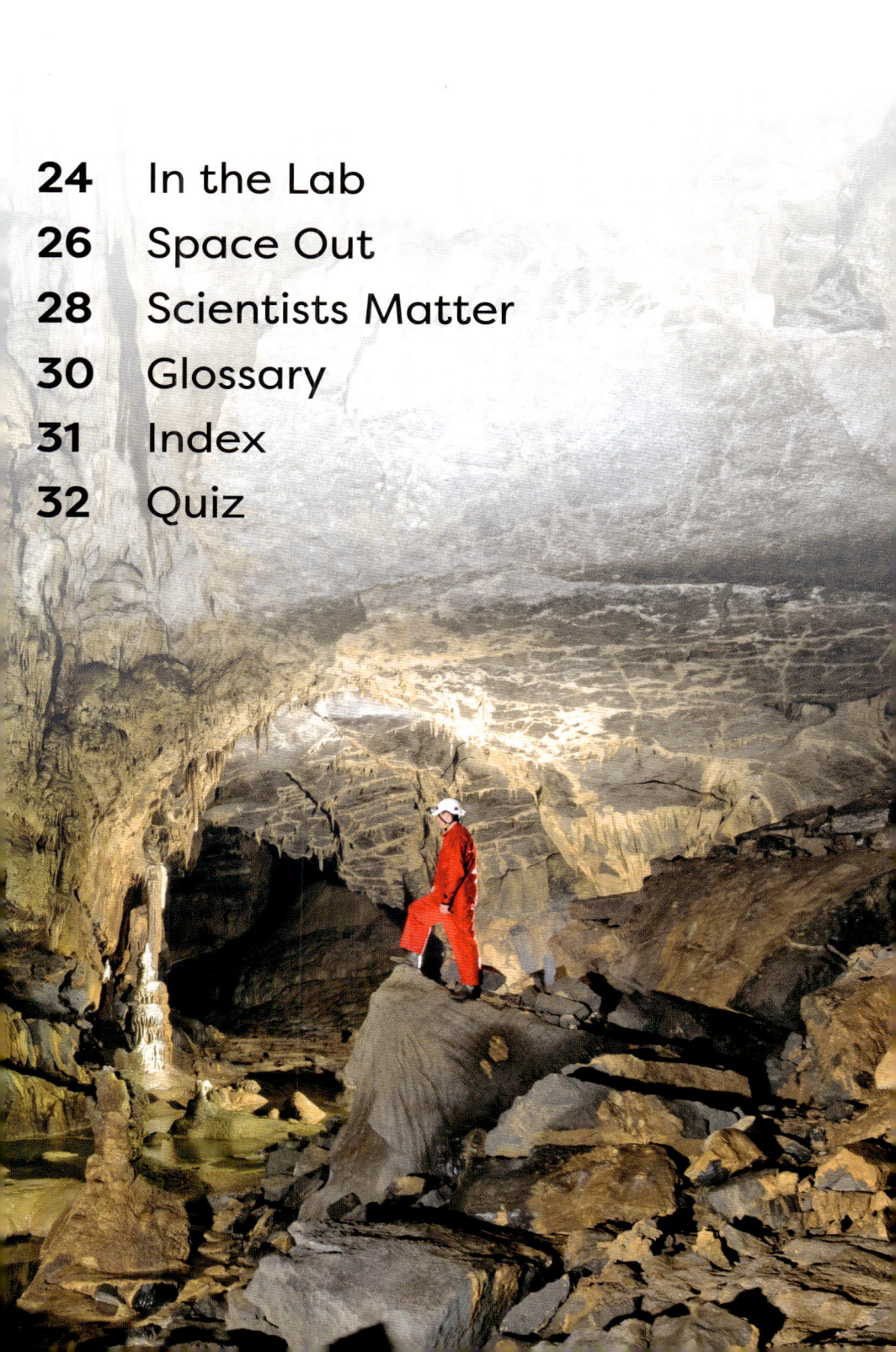

What Does a Scientist Do?

Scientists study many things.

Scientists study animals and plants. They learn about the weather and Earth.

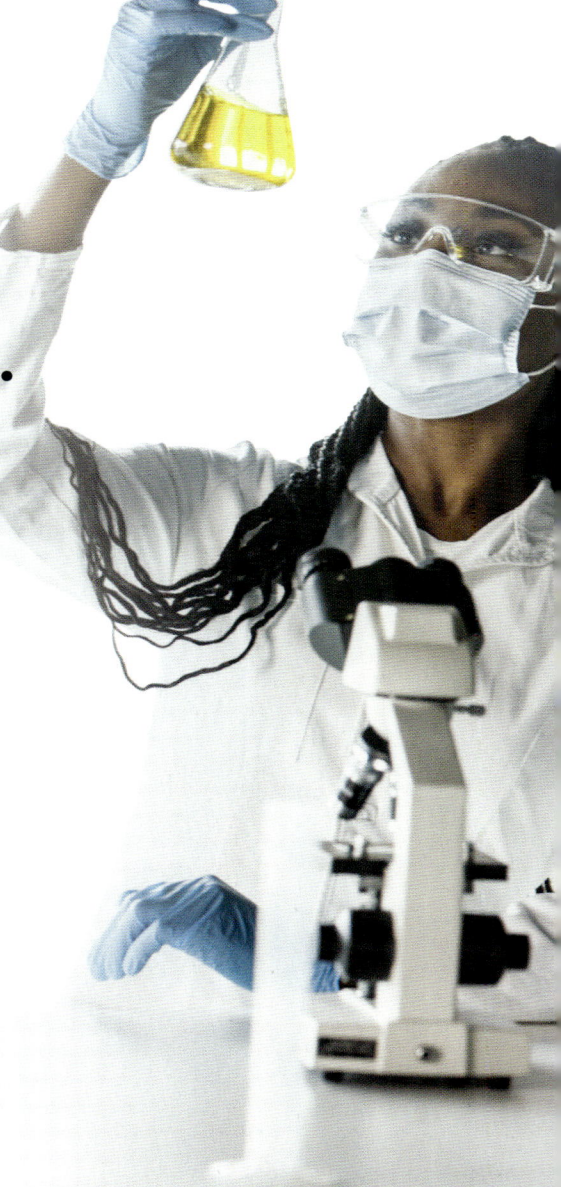

Scientists gather facts.
Scientific facts are
called data.
Scientists write about
what they learn.
They share what
they learn.
They use the data
to solve problems.
Sometimes, what they
learn makes them ask
more questions.

Where Does a Scientist Work?

Scientists work everywhere. Some scientists work outside. This scientist studies rivers and streams.

Many
scientists
work inside.
They work in labs
and hospitals.
These scientists
study diseases.
Their work helps to make
new kinds of medicine.

What Does a Scientist Need?

Scientists go to school. They learn how to observe.

Scientists use special gear.

This scientist uses ropes to climb. He counts the eggs in the nest. Special gear helps keep this scientist safe.

This scientist uses a microscope. She looks at very tiny things.

Many scientists take pictures. They make notes and draw pictures. A computer helps keep track of data they collect.

Let's Get to Work!

Scientists work in different places. They walk, drive, ride, or fly to work.

Some scientists work in places where there are no roads. Some hike into mountains.

These scientists travel across the snow.

Life on Earth

Many scientists study animals. They study things animals do. They learn what animals eat.

This scientist learns about moose families.

These scientists carefully clear away the dirt. They dig out a dinosaur fossil. They learn about animals that lived very long ago.

Scientists learn how plants grow.
This helps us grow more food to eat.

Scientists learn about plants in the wild. They study the giant trees in this forest. These trees create homes for other plants and animals.

Weather Watch

Scientists learn about different kinds of weather. They track rain, snow, and storms.
This helps people plan. It keeps them safe.

Scientists study how weather changes. This scientist measures the wind. She will compare it to the wind from last year.

Down to Earth

Scientists study Earth.
They want to know how
Earth formed.
Many learn about rocks.
They make maps of
where to find different
kinds of rocks.
This helps people know
where to build roads
or houses.

These scientists work
deep in a cave.
They discover new things
to study.

Scientists study how Earth changes. Earthquakes make the ground shake.

Big earthquakes can knock down buildings. Scientists figure out how to plan for them.

Scientists learn about volcanoes.
These scientists study how lava flows.
They use the facts to keep people safe.

In the Lab

Many scientists work in a laboratory. The lab has special equipment. They do experiments here.

Scientists study water. They find ways to keep it clean.

They study the human body. They learn how to keep people healthy.

Many scientists think of new ways to use computers.

This scientist studies how geckos climb walls. He uses the data to make robots that can climb.

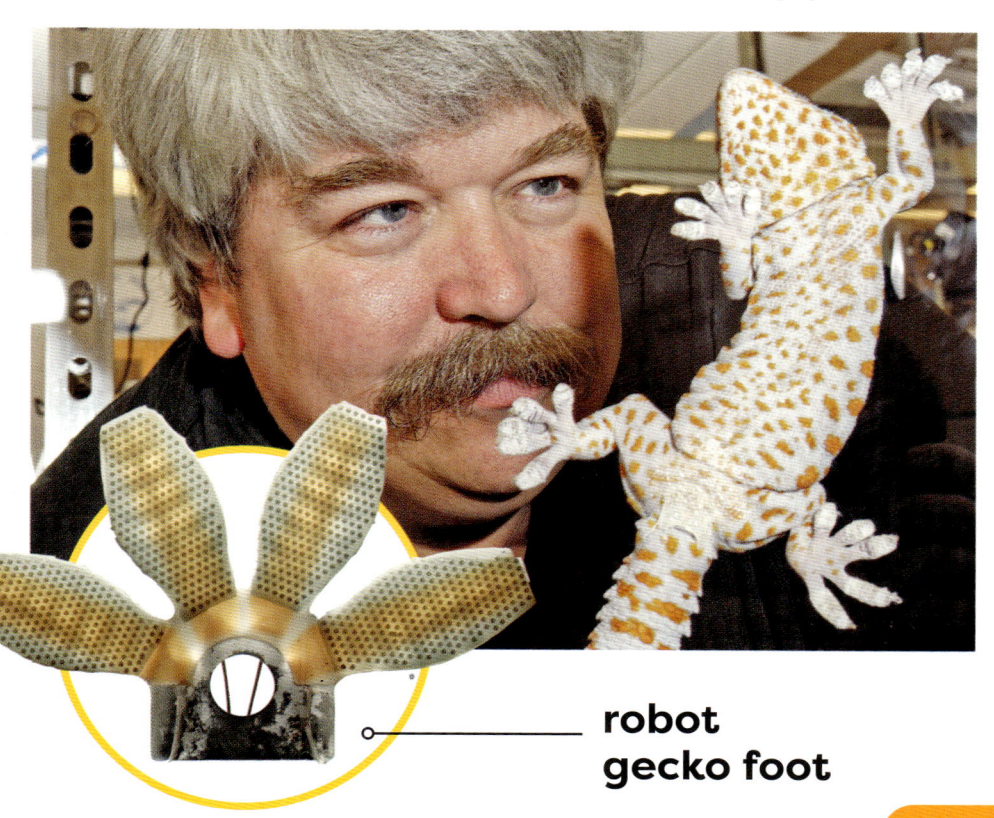

robot gecko foot

Space Out

Scientists study space.
They learn about planets
that are far away.

This scientist looks far
out in space.
She studies the stars.

These scientists make new tools. Scientists will use these tools to explore Earth's moon.

Some scientists live in space. They gather data about life in space. This will help future scientists travel far out in space.

Scientists Matter

Scientists are curious. They want to learn more about the world. Every day, scientists learn something new.

Scientists find ways to
help cure illnesses.
They think of new ways
to grow food.
They help us plan for
bad weather.
Their discoveries help
people, animals,
and the planet.

Glossary

data
facts scientists collect and study

experiment
a scientific test to see what happens under different conditions

laboratory
a room with equipment to do science experiments

microscope
a tool that magnifies/ makes small things look larger

volcano
an opening in Earth's crust where lava flows out

Index

 Quiz

Answer the questions to see what you have learned. Check your answers with an adult.

1. What happens in an earthquake?

2. What is a word that can describe a scientist?

3. Name three things scientists study.

4. True or False: Scientists use computers.

5. How do scientists learn about weather?

1. The ground shakes 2. Curious 3. Plants, animals, weather, Earth, space 4. True 5. They track storms